MONEY
$ecret$!

JJ DeSpain

PUBLICATIONS INTERNATIONAL, LTD.

JJ DeSpain writes about health, consumerism, and senior issues for national magazines in the United States and Canada. She is a former critical care nurse and has had a variety of experiences working with and for various government groups, including the Veterans Administration. She is co-author of *Government Secrets* and author of *Life-Saving Health Secrets, Inside Info,* and *Everyday Antiques*.

Additional editorial assistance: Phyllis Schomaker

ISBN: 0-7853-5154-X

Contents

Introduction

Getting and Holding on to More Money

We love our money. That's why we spend more than 40 years as adults working for it, spending it, and investing it. We look for ways to make it grow, keep it safe, and hide it from the tax collector. We stash it away for a vacation, college, and a new car.

Have you ever thought about the extent to which money dictates your life? You probably never step outside without having some in your pocket. It's responsible for where you eat dinner: at a fine restaurant or a fast-food outlet. It decides whether you use public transportation, drive an old beater, or zip around in a fancy SUV.

And it determines the kind of health care you receive. In one form or another, money is behind most political promises and skirmishes.

Money is definitely at the root of your life, liberty, and pursuit of happiness. You learn that the first time you earn an allowance or when the tooth fairy leaves a buck or two for your incisor. But most of us can use a little help managing that buck.

All money comes shrouded in secrets, but nobody's sharing these secrets because they don't care what you spend. It's not *their* money. And they benefit if you're not on top of your game, if you don't know all the tips and tricks that help you manage your money better.

Money and its many aspects weave through just about everything in our lives. It's online in the form of schemes, scams, banking, and buying. It's on TV in infomercials, investments, and insurance. Listen to the radio. Look at a billboard. Everyone wants your money, and many of them have some secrets up their sleeves to charm it right out of you. But now, in *Money Secrets! Hundreds of Ways to Make, Save & Find Money!* you can find out what they know, learn their inside money secrets, and develop a few secret money-saving strategies of your own. You'll pick up a few ideas that can transform your time and talent into extra income, as well as tap into your house for spare change. And you'll learn how to protect your bucks, how to spot the scammers, and where to go for help.

In the physical realm, money doesn't literally make the world go around. But knowing more about it can sure make your own private world a better place in which to live. After all, it's *your* money. Shouldn't you be the one to control it?

Chapter 1

Easy Money in Your Pocket

Would you like to scratch up a few unexpected dollars for doing something simple that you enjoy? Here are a few easy-earning ideas you'll wish you'd thought of years ago. They will point you in unexpected directions that have never occurred to you before.

Bargains Galore!

Want to get the most out of your garage sale? Here's how.

• Advertise in the newspaper a day prior to as well as the day of your sale.

• In your ad, list the sure-fire thing that'll drag in the big spenders—antiques! But make sure you actually have a few to stick in the sale.

• Price to sell. If you think you can get $10 for it, price it at $7.50 to guarantee that sale.

• Offer discounts. Fill up a half-off box or give 10 percent off anything. Customers always buy more when they think they're getting a bargain.

• Near the end of the sale, slash prices even more.

• Display prices on signs and by location rather than putting individual stickers on every item. A sign that says "Shirts 50¢, Pants 75¢" takes only minutes to make—tagging each item could take hours.

• At the end of the day, to clean out items not yet sold, make offers such as "$1.00 for everything that can fit in a grocery bag." This often spurs a spending spree.

Dealing With the Flea People

Flea markets are a good way to dispose of just about anything. Setting up in one is pretty inexpensive, sometimes as little as $75 for a two- or three-day weekend. But there are some setting-up tips you should know that will pay off in bigger profits.

Fast Fact

If you really love those garage sales, plan them for others. The overhead is cheap. All you need are business cards and price tags. Post flyers on grocery store bulletin boards for people to hire you to set up and price their garage sale. For your efforts you can claim up to 25 percent of the take. Best times: spring and fall.

• Take your own table. Flea marketeers will rent tables to you, but they can cost nearly as much as the booth space.

• Get a corner location for double the exposure.

• Stay away from food areas. People mingle there, blocking real shoppers.

• If you're selling vintage merchandise, insist on space in an area with similar goods. Nice old kitchenware between two booths selling tractor parts won't be noticed.

• Don't forget all those tax-deductible expenses. If you're earning money, all your expenses become write-offs: entrance fees, lunch, and even gas mileage become taxable deductions.

• Keep a supply of business cards on display at your booth. People may remember your wares and call you later if they are unsure of making an on-the-spot purchase.

A Hunting You Will Go

For what? How about forgotten stocks, bonds, certificates, deeds, or other important papers that might be worth money. Friends or relatives who have passed away may have hidden papers in a "safe place" and then never told anyone!

First, look in the obvious places:
• drawers
• boxes
• chests
• jewelry boxes

Next, start the real search:
• taped behind pictures
• underneath drawers
• taped to the thin, flat board separating drawers in antique dressers
• under furniture
• in photo albums and old books
• under loose floor boards
• in the backs of large clocks
• taped inside a piano lid

Bedrooms are the most likely areas to search, followed by dens and other rooms in which the person spent time alone. Kitchens are a less likely place to find the goods, but if the person hiding them was devious, try the kitchen.

Those Who Can Do Also Teach

There's someone out there who would pay to know what you know or to be able to do what you do. So take advantage and become a teacher. You could teach skills that seem to be lost to new generations, like crocheting, knitting, soap-making, whittling, painting, or quilting. If you've ever made anything, you can probably teach someone else how to do it, too. You don't need a degree. You don't even need much experience. Here are some teaching places that are just waiting for your skill:

• Continuing education classes at your local university—they're open to just about anything of interest.

• Local companies or corporations—they're always on the lookout for business education classes, such as business writing.

Here's what you can expect to be paid:
• continuing education class—$25-$30/hour
• corporation or company—$30-$50/hour

Some at-your-convenience teaching opportunities:

• Do you have a teaching certificate? Check for home-schooling organizations in your area and make your services available. Most communities require that licensed teachers look in on home-school progress from time to time.

• Got an athletic skill? Many schools hire coaches from the outside. No, you won't get the football or basketball team, but you could get the volleyball or tennis team. If you have expertise, call several local schools and let them know you're available.

• Tutor, anyone? If you have the expertise, some failing student needs it. Get your credentials together and take them to a local principal or the head of a school's department in which you hope to tutor.

Another Teaching Gig

Have you ever considered being a substitute teacher? There are some advantages:

• Many states do not require a full four-year teaching degree. Some will accept only two years.

• You can work on the days you choose.

• For Social Security recipients, the amount you're allowed to earn without losing your benefits grows all the time. Don't worry about earning too much.

• You'll have no lesson plans to prepare or papers to grade.

• You can feel free to turn down an offer if the timing is inconvenient or the assignment is not of your preference. Repeated refusals, however, may result in placement at the bottom of the district's call list.

• A day's pay can average $65 for a shift that ends in the early afternoon. Not bad as supplemental or extra income.

Check with your local board of education to see what they require in a substitute teacher, then add your name to the list. If you prefer parochial schools, call for the same information.

Earn Extra Income From Writing, Editing, Research, or Publishing

If you've been told you have a way with words or you love to entertain with your stories, consider using those skills to pick up some extra bucks. The most costly overhead is paper and postage. You might want to take a refresher course or browse through a copy of *Writer's Market* or back issues of *Writer's Digest* magazine in your local library. Then sit yourself at your desk and put your ideas on paper.

Need Some Free Time Away From Home?

Sure you do, especially when the price tag adds up to zero.

• Do you love a cool ocean breeze? Then recruit all your friends for a cruise and call a travel agency. The gang leader of 20 or more sea cruisers usually gets free passage.

• When you step off the boat, herd those 20 friends over to Amtrak for a rail vacation, and as gang leader, you'll get a free ticket there, too.

• Like to dance? If you're a mature, single man and don't mind escorting unattached, single women, most cruise lines need your services and will give you the trip for free.

Travel as an Air Courier

Air couriers have a chance to see exotic places often beyond their budgets. Many companies prefer to send freight through as luggage rather than shipping it as air cargo. Courier trips are usually for seven days, but some are 10, 14, and 21 days, or even up to six months. Your discounted flight can cost $50-$150 for international travel to places like Brazil and China. Free flights are occasionally offered, and super-discounted, last-minute flights are common. You don't have to actually carry anything, but you may have to give up part or all of your luggage allowance. For information, check the Web site www.courier.org or contact: The International Association of Air Travel Couriers, P.O. Box 1349, Lake Worth, Florida 33460.

You can also call them at 561-582-8320 or e-mail iaatc@courier.org.

My House Is Your House

For the adventure lover, swapping houses can be an inexpensive way to vacation in destinations you never thought you could afford. You get to spend a week in someone else's Colorado ski-country home while they stay in your Florida beach house. And you'll save as much as $100 per day over the cost of a hotel vacation. There are hundreds of house-swapping opportunities available on the Internet, under the keywords *home exchange*, but be cautious.

• Correspond with your swap-mate several times to get a feel for who will be sleeping in your bed.

• Make sure your homeowners insurance will cover your guest. If your car is part of the deal, be sure to check your auto policy, too.

• Ask for references, especially from a previous exchange partner.

• Draw up a trade agreement outlining responsibilities and limitations for both parties.

Bed & Breakfast Bucks

Does your house seem like a country inn? Do you have a couple of extra rooms you rarely use? If there's any reason why people come to visit your neck of the woods, hang out a bed & breakfast shingle. Here are some B&B tidbits to consider.

• An average B&B room brings in about $65 per night, but to grab patrons, be sure you don't charge more than nearby hotels and motels.

• Most B&Bs have only a 33-percent-occupancy rate, so don't count your dollars until they hatch.

- B&Bs traditionally open only on weekends.

- You'll have out-of-pocket expenses: laundry, breakfast food, insurance.

Let Your House Earn a Living

Is your house haunted? Does your old Victorian have a spectacular stained-glass window? Maybe the seascape view from your cottage is breathtaking. Whatever the case, if your house, or any portion of it, stands out in a crowd, it could earn you some movie, commercial, or TV money. Here's what you do:

- Take 5×7 color photos of your house, with all the intricate architectural and scenic details.

- Compose a written description for each photo.

Low-Cost B&B Advertising

An advertising budget can kill your B&B profits, so advertise on the cheap. Make up brochures and distribute them to nearby corporations, universities (for visiting faculty and parents), hospitals, and tourist attractions.

Take a peek at these references for more information and to find out how to get an inexpensive national listing in each (both are updated frequently):

- Bed and Breakfast U.S.A. by Peggy Ackerman, published by Plume

- America's Favorite Inns, B&Bs & Small Hotels by Sandra W. Soule, published by St. Martin's Press

- Write down interesting, attention-grabbing facts about your house—its history or articles about it in a newspaper or magazine.

- Combine everything into a folder and send it, with a cover letter, to the film office in your state. Every state has one, so you can look it up in your phone book.

- Be sure to get all the media attention you can muster for your house's specialty. Many film commissions offer programs to help promote film opportunities.

Did George Washington Really Sleep There?

People will pay to see that, if you can prove it. If your home is historic or the kind people just want to take a peek into, maybe they'll plunk down $4 or $5 for a tour. To become a tourist attraction:

- Check with your local government for licensing.

- Get adequate insurance.

- Print up brochures, then let your local tourist bureau know you're open for business.

- Ask to include your brochure in the tourist information racks in hotels.

- If your house is certifiably historic, ask your state historical society what it takes to be included in the National Register of Historic Places.

- Find out more about your house. Search the title history at your city hall or county courthouse. A few phone calls will determine who holds the records: try the assessor's office, the recorder of deeds, then the archives within that department. Once you have the names of past owners, check for information about these people in the local genealogy section of your main library.

• And don't forget—beautiful gardens and large rooms are sought after for weddings and receptions. Consider renting them out.

What Else Is Around Town?

Own a van, minivan, or travel home? Become a tour guide in your own town or in a city you love to visit, and share your knowledge and enthusiasm with others. Check out prices of current tours, and charge a per-capita rate of whatever the market will accept. You might want to include a lunch for an extra fee and either pack it along or arrange with nearby restaurants for a group rate. Be sure to check with local authorities for information about permits, licenses, or usage fees.

Easy Cash for Stashing Their Stuff

You know that empty room in your basement? Rent it out. Rent out that empty minibarn, too, or the half of the garage you're not using. People need more space, and if you have it, they'll pay you to store something in it. Here's the way to do it:

• Consult your insurance agent to determine any liability and insurance needs.

• Check out prices at local storage complexes.

• Undercut the competition since you won't be offering the services they do, such as 24-hour access.

• Advertise on bulletin boards in grocery stores, and pass out flyers in nearby apartment complexes.

• Make sure your space renters won't want to visit their stuff too often.

• On a smaller scale, put a few lockers in a garage or basement space to store smaller valuables and papers for people.

—Insurance companies recommend that everyone keep duplicates of documents and pictures at a separate location than the originals, as backup in case of fire or other catastrophe.

—Businesses use remote storage facilities for computer backup files as well.

—The going rates should be similar to rent for a safe deposit box, but add on a few dollars if you can handle pickup and delivery services.

—If you plan to keep photographic materials, you'll need to maintain proper humidity and temperature control.

A Little More Cash-Cow Space

If that extra space happens to be a furnished bedroom or a room over the garage, take in a renter.

• Check newspaper listings for the going room rental rate in your area. Make sure your rental charge includes additional cost on your homeowners policy and additional use of utilities.

• Ask for a security deposit to cover unexpected expenses or possible damages to your property.

• Renter meals are *not* included, but you can work out a meal deal with a renter to put a little extra dough in your pocket.

• Your phone is also not included in the deal. You can relent on local calls if your service isn't measured, but don't allow long-distance calls unless you work out some type of agreement with your renter.

• If washer-and-dryer use is included, renters must use their own laundry supplies.

• List yourself with local churches, colleges, and other organizations. Newspaper ads can be risky and draw some undesirables to your door. Some colleges have student housing referral services.

• Be sure to establish your house rules in writing regarding such things as smoking, visitors, noise, and cleanliness from the beginning.

• Don't forget the tax advantages. The percentage of space you rent out allows you to deduct that same percentage from your total house upkeep, including utilities, taxes, and general repairs. Any furnishings specifically supplied to the rented space are 100 percent deductible.

The Seeds of Extra Cash

Gardening is on the rise again, and those who aren't doing it sure wish they could. That's where you can come in.

• If you have a large yard or lot, rent out garden plots. Pass out flyers to apartment dwellers and anyone else in the neighborhood who lives on a postage-stamp-size parcel.

• Sell produce from your own garden. Tack a sign to your fence post that will let everyone know what you're selling. Make sure you're open at the same time every day. Undercut supermarket prices. Make your display look plentiful—buyers like that.

• If you live near a vacant lot owned by the local

government, ask permission to use it, for free, for a community garden. Permission is often granted.

• If you have limited space, consider growing herbs for teas, medicinal use, crafting, or cooking. Health food stores often love to obtain fresh, homegrown leaves and seeds to sell.

• Flowers have uses even after they've wilted. Set up a drying rack and come up with your own recipes for potpourri using favorite blooms from your garden. Make dried flower arrangements and wreaths, or sell the raw products to craft stores.

Love to Cook?

Put it to use. Many people are in need of a good home-cooked meal, and it doesn't have to be fancy. Just stir up some extra portions of what you're cooking for the day. Here's what you do:

• Decide which meal will be the easiest to prepare and deliver.

• Set your prices modestly. People who will use this service are usually in financial need.

• Contact area churches, neighborhood associations, and senior citizens centers.

• Prepare extra freezer meals for days you don't want to cook yourself.

• Utilize your grocery-store skills to get the best deals. (See Chapter 5.)

And Don't Forget Fluffy & Fido

Pets aren't cheap to keep if you're a responsible pet owner. But there are some critter cost cutters that will help keep those doggone dollars in your pocket.

- Switch to dry food. Vitamins and nutrients are the same, but you'll get 50 percent or more for your dollar.

- Invest $30 in grooming tools (make sure you buy a kit with a how-to video), and do the grooming yourself. Be sure you also buy a $5, hard-plastic wading pool for bathing your pet. You'll save about $30 for each grooming trip you don't need to take.

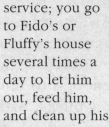

- Look into pet health insurance. If Fluffy has a chronic problem, it will be worth the cost. Ask your vet for details.

- Grow your own catnip.

- Negotiate service prices for necessities like surgery, or for discounts if you take more than one pet to the same vet.

Pet Sitting

You might be surprised what people will pay to have someone look in on or care for their loved ones. Other people's Fluffys and Fidos can mean money in your doggie bag.

- Start up a vacation service; you go to Fido's or Fluffy's house several times a day to let him out, feed him, and clean up his messes. Cats can be visited less frequently.

- Start a daily in-home visit service for pet owners who work.

- Do you have facilities for overnight four-legged guests? Many pet owners would be happier to have Fluffy in a real home instead of in a kennel when they are out of town for a few days.

Chapter 2

Collectibles and Crafts for Cash

An antique is something old, right? Sort of. But age doesn't always determine what's collectible and what's not. You could be lucky enough to find stuff that others will buy for big bucks. Barbies, baseball cards, and stamps are obvious collectibles. But glassware, toys, and Christmas ornaments can be collectibles, too. The range of what these items might be worth can be from nothing to thousands of dollars. When you look at what you've got, as well as what you might make with your own hands, you could find a whole new income!

Search Everywhere

Look around the basement, the attic, and the garage for possible antiques and collectibles. Don't overlook the obvious. The clock or the painting passed down through the family that's sitting right in your living room could be priceless. Look for anything from your childhood or older, for things that appeal to you, and for weird things. Some elements to look for include:

- trademarks
- signatures
- logos
- brand names

Identify any categories your newfound treasure might fit into, such as the following:

- advertising: movie posters, beer ads, etc.
- animation characters
- art
- autographs
- barbershop and shaving paraphernalia
- bottles: for medicines or tonics, Log Cabin syrup bottles
- clocks, timepieces: preferably still working, engraving a bonus
- collector plates
- comic books
- cultural: anything Shaker, Native American, Pennsylvania Dutch, etc.
- hobbies: such as model railroad accessories and trains
- lunch boxes: preferably old metal ones, especially with thermos intact
- military items
- music boxes: especially those made in Germany
- Pez candy dispensers
- political campaign paraphernalia: the older or more remote, the better
- royal commemorative: not only Diana, but anything with a royal connection
- snowglobes
- souvenirs: from events, the older the better, and places, especially ones that are gone now
- tobacco products: pipes, humidors, cigarette cases, lighters, and even ashtrays

- tools: especially hand-made; even old nails and hinges
- vanity items: nonsynthetic bristle brushes, particularly items that are hand-painted or gilded
- vintage items: from the turn of the century or a world's fair
- vintage sewing: thimbles, darning equipment, pincushions, sewing baskets

Consider it a bonus if any of your items fit into one or more categories. If you have a Mickey Mouse lunch box, you can appeal to collectors from both the animation and lunch box camps.

Do some research in your collectible categories at the library or on the Internet. Television shows such as *Antiques Roadshow, Appraisal Fair*, and *Appraise It!* not only inform, they entertain and encourage, as well.

If programs like this aren't available in your area, you can always check out the Web. These television shows have sites that offer greater detail about the items featured on their programs as well as referrals to other information about collectibles. Surf over to the *Antiques Roadshow* site at www.pbs.org/wgbh/pages/roadshow and to *Appraisal Fair* and *Appraise It!* at hgtv.com/HGTV. While you're online, also take a look at eBay, www.ebay.com, to browse their categories and see how your items might fit.

What's It Worth?

The resources above can help you find out what your stash might be worth. Make note cards listing the lowest and highest prices you've seen charged for the items you've found. Books and other resources estimate their prices based on the top prices paid, so you should not expect to get that much. On the other hand, if you find a collector who needs your piece to complete a collection, you could cash in big time.

Look on auction Web sites, such as eBay, and see the final prices bid for items similar to yours. It has happened, for instance, that the same Donald Duck cookie jar went for both $99 and $15 to different bidders on different days. Why?

• Condition, condition, condition. It's everything.

• Items still in their original packaging are worth more.

• Items that haven't been repaired or changed are worth more.

If you think your antique is of great value, have it appraised. Contact the American Society of Appraisers for a certified appraisal expert in your area at www.appraisers.org or 703-478-2228.

Selling at Antique Malls and Flea Markets

You've reached the point where you have more collectibles and antiques than you can use, swap, or store. Or maybe you just want to "liquidate your assets" and turn them into cash. It's time to go professional. You might not want to rent a store and jump right into a deal with a lot of overhead and investment, so consider setting up shop in an antique or collectibles mall or a flea market. The basics are the same, but antique malls offer a more permanent location while flea markets tend to be short-term affairs. In many antique malls, you will be able to set up your display and check in with the mall sales personnel from time to time, but at the flea market, you are your own (and maybe only) salesperson.

Before you load up the truck and head to the mall or the flea market:

• Scout your area antique malls and flea markets. Consider how far you're willing to travel for a flea market. Look for the sites that are busy, convenient, and advertised well. You might benefit from amenities like snack bars, rest rooms, and ATMs, which can sometimes encourage customers to stay longer. Every parent with small kids in tow knows they will undoubtedly leave early if there are no bathrooms.

• You can find a list of flea markets in your area by checking the classified ads

in your local newspaper or on the Web at www. fleamarketguide.com.

• Plan your setup and how you will display your wares. Try to make it as attractive and unique as possible. Find a way to spotlight your hot items. Don't be afraid to borrow ideas from other success-ful booths you've seen while visiting for research.

• Inventory your goods. Make sure you have enough to offer.

• Be sure your pricing is competitive yet profitable.

• Find ways to promote yourself, such as advertis-ing on your own. At the market, set up an interac-tive feature, a contest, or a freebie to draw attention from the crowd.

• You need to know the rules about late arrival or no-shows, banned items, restrictions on signs, parking, animals, insurance requirements, and required licenses.

• Watch out for hidden fees for things like
    —security
    —electricity
    —advertising
    —use of tables or equipment
    —tax permits
    —cleanup

Online Auctions

Here's another potential forum for you to market your collectibles. Online auctions provide a lot of services and have a huge customer base. If your collectibles are large or breakable, you will have some shipping issues to consider. But you spend little time and effort once your listing is set up, and you lose nothing if your items don't sell. Shopping online is easy for the buyer as well, which increases the likelihood of sales. Buyers have no traveling to do, can browse at their leisure, must pay no entry fees, and can go to the bathroom whenever they want.

Before jumping in, take some time to check the

Branching Out

The secret to any successful sale is to buy low and sell high. Of course your own stuff is already yours, but once you become savvy, you can branch out into buying and selling. Peruse other sales in your area, and take notes on the hot items people are seeking. Become a know-it-all, starting in one area at a time. The best way to find a bargain is to know its worth—especially when the seller doesn't.

Research one field, such as porcelain, crystal, or soft-drink collectibles, and start making purchases for resale.

water. Browse auction sites and their listings to see who else is selling items similar to yours. It's just another way to know your competition.

This is how online auctions work.

• You'll need to register, but no problem, it's free. However, you will need to provide credit-card information to verify your identity and demonstrate that you are serious. Your credit card company will also provide you with added protection against loss or theft.

• You will have options as to how you accept payment from bidders.

—Most sites offer themselves as go-betweens for a small fee ranging from 35 cents to between 1½

and 2½ percent of the final selling price.

—You can deal directly with buyers yourself, if you like. But don't ship anything to a buyer until the check clears. You have little recourse if you get ripped off. In many instances, you can do no more than warn future victims and give the cheater a bad online reputation.

• Write a full description of your item(s), including defects, markings, special features, and details. Explain your intended shipping method and if shipping charges will be added to the buyer's cost.

Include a good picture of your item. The Web site will have instructions for how to do this.

• Sales tax and income tax are your responsibilities.

Check with your local government about the regulations in your state.

• Choose categories in which to list your collectibles.

• The auction Web site may charge you a fee of between 30 cents and $3.30, depending on the opening bid, to list your item, and a final selling fee, usually 1¼ to 5 percent of the official selling price.

Selling to the Dealers

Now, this can be tricky, because most antiques and collectibles dealers are more than happy to take advantage of you when they can. You've already done your research, so you know what they might be worth. That's the best information you can have as you go in. Here are some more deal-making defenses.

• Expect to receive about 50 to 75 percent of the appraisal or book price when you sell.

• Never accept the first offer. Ask for more.

Going...Going...Gone...

To the auction. Unless you have a valuable piece that will sell in a specialty auction, such as antiques or art, chances are an auction house is not the best place to sell. Why? You'll have to pay an auction house fee, which can be as much as 50 percent for a single item, or 33 percent or more for several items. Before you cart that old taxidermied beaver off to the auction, know the auction house's terms.

• Offer your object to several different dealers and grab the best price.

• If you haven't had an appraisal and the offers are consistently more than you thought your antique was worth, don't sell. Get it appraised!

When That Crafting Bug Bites

Antiques and collectibles aren't the only items that you can put out on the market. If you've just got to keep making crafts, and if your end result so far is a closetful of crafts that have no home, you may have found another potential business. Here are some ways to sell the fruits of your crafty labors.

• Find space in a craft mall. They're springing up all over the country, and all you have to do is rent booth space and set up your displays. Store personnel will see to the sales. Some antique malls accept craft displays, too.

• Sell through an in-home sale, similar to a garage sale. Advertise it as a craft show. The best time is before Christmas.

• Investigate geezer.com, pardon the name. It's a free online service where seniors can list and sell their crafts.

• The "ize" have it—special*ize*, advert*ize*, capital*ize*. Start with only a few items or categories that you do well. Pay attention to those that might be unique to the market or that seem promising as best-sellers.

• Look for craft fairs in your town and find out how to get involved. Displaying your work at these events provides great exposure.

Chapter 3

The Government Giveth

Good old Uncle Sam. He's always standing there with his hand out, ready to take. But take a peek in his other hand. You might just find a little something there that can help your money situation in ways you never expected.

Money for Something You Love to Do

Uncle Sam has finally seen the worth of writers and is handing out money to writers of prose and poetry. The criteria for receiving a literature fellowship are artistic excellence and literary merit.

Past recipients have received free, no-payback money for such projects as putting poetry on posters in buses, so if you think your work will pass the test, find out the specifics from arts.endow.gov on the Web or from: Office of Communications, National Endowment for the Arts, Washington, DC 20506-0001; 202-682-5428.

Earn Money by Alphabetizing

Want to help preserve some history? The National Endowment for the Humanities has grant money for anyone who can create and carry out a project to aid in maintaining important national research collections. And the good news is, the work can be fun. Recent projects have included:

• preserving photos relating to the history of the railroad

• conducting a preservation assessment of a famous American artist

• arranging storage and housing for a textile and costume collection

For more information, e-mail preservation@neh.gov or visit www.neh.gov/whoweare/overview.html.

Just Can't Get Enough of the Humanities?

Let that passion find some free money for you. Come up with an idea to help create knowledge in the humanities. Previous projects have included:

• Creating a searchable database of contemporary disabled writers.

• Writing on the American folk aspects of Aaron Copland's music.

• Translating papers written during the Holocaust.

You can:

• Apply for a fellowship that will give you grant money, for up to a year, to undertake full-time independent study. E-mail fellowships@neh.gov or visit www.neh.gov/whoweare/overview.html for more information.

• Go after a part-time summer study grant, called a summer stipend, that will keep your nose to the grindstone for only two months. E-mail stipends@neh.gov or see www.neh.gov/whoweare/overview.html if you're interested.

Three Years of Free Moolah

More with the humanities, and it can be a cash cow for someone with the right education, knowledge, or background. This grant money is specifically for research in the preparation for publication of:

• editions
• translations
• other important works in the humanities

The money will trickle into your pockets for up to three years. For further information, e-mail

research@neh.gov or, once again, visit www.neh.gov/whoweare/overview.html.

Do You Love to Teach?

If you have the academic credentials, there's a university ready and eager to give you grant money, and all you have to do is conduct a seminar, institute, or workshop. The sky's the limit when it comes to topics.

For more information, e-mail sem-inst@neh.gov or go online to www.neh.gov/whoweare/overview.html.

This Will Help Preserve Your Financial Heritage

Preserving our cultural heritage is so high on Uncle Sam's "to do" list that he has another chance for you to help him in exchange for some free bucks. Here's how you can cash in:

Fast Fact

Government grants are a great way to find money for doing things you love to do, but every grant has a yearly application deadline, so check it out before you apply.

- Put on a festival, exhibit, or other preservation project that increases the public's appreciation for our cultural traditions.

- Serve an apprenticeship to pass cultural traditions on to future generations.

- Document, record, or conserve significant cultural works or collections of art or artifacts.

To find out how to pocket some of this money, go to www.arts.gov, or write to: National Endowment for the Arts, 1100 Pennsylvania Ave NW, Washington, DC 20506.

Uncle Sam, M.D.

Health care isn't cheap these days. But don't despair. The government sponsors more than 5,000 clinical trials at any given time, and you might qualify for some free medical attention. Uncle Sam has an eye out for women to participate in research for

That Time of the Year

You sneeze, cough, wheeze, and ache everywhere but your eyelids, which means it's flu season again. Did you know that:

- Flu kills 20,000 people every year?

- Pneumonia is responsible for snuffing out another 70,000 lives?

If you have Medicare Part B, Uncle Sam will pay for the flu and pneumonia shots that protect you. Here's where you can usually find the needle:
- your doctor
- pharmacy flu shot clinics
- VA medical centers (only for veterans)
- community and senior citizens' centers

For more information, call 800-633-4227 or go to www.medicare.gov.

female-associated conditions. If you qualify, here are some of the perks:

• free screenings and exams
• access to new drugs and medical procedures
• free treatment
• stipend or travel expenses for many programs

For a list of current clinical trials and application guidelines, visit clinicaltrials.gov or write to: U.S. National Library of Medicine, NLM Customer Service, 8600 Rockville Pike, Bethesda, MD 20894.

They Won't Give You a Naval Vessel

But you could get some free stuff if your nonprofit organization needs:

• office machines
• furniture
• motor vehicles
• clothing

• construction equipment
• medical supplies
• boats
• airplanes
• communication equipment

The government operates a program that allows certain nonfederal organizations to obtain property that's no longer in use. To see if your organization qualifies, and to find out how to take advantage of this giveaway, contact: Central Office, General Services Administration, Federal Supply Service, 1941 Jefferson Davis Highway, Room 812, Arlington, VA 22202; 703-305-7240. Ask for the address and phone number of your regional office, then contact them.

Who Owes You?

If you don't know, they won't tell you. So, check

these out for bucks that could be rightfully yours.

• Your state unclaimed property office. Find the phone number in your phone book's government pages.

• If you had a HUD/FHA insured mortgage, go to the refund checker at www.hud.gov/fha/comp/refunds/page1.html, or call 800-697-6967.

• Do you think you are owed some pension funds?

Fast Fact

The IRS has a freebie for you. It will let you off the penalty hook if you're a late tax filer. But look out if you're about to hit the three-years-late mark. After three years, you don't get your refund back. That's the law, and each year about $2 billion in refunds are lost under these regulations. Ouch!

Start your search at search.pbgc.gov/srchname.cfm or write to: PBGC Pension Search Program, 1200 K Street NW, Washington, DC 20005.

• Did your credit union go belly up? You could have something coming if it did. To find out, go to www.ncua.gov/news/unclaimed/unclaimed.html.

• Are you or a close family member a Holo-

Attention All Veterans

Do you have some cash coming to you? Statistics show that only 11 percent of all World War I, World War II, and Korean Conflict vets are cashing in on their benefits, including pensions. So you'd better check it out. For more information, call 800-827-1000, or contact your local Veterans Affairs office. Look in your phone book's government pages or visit www.va.gov for the VA location nearest you.

caust survivor? To see if you have restitution money coming, go to the Claims Conference Restitution Guide at www. claimscon.org/guide.html, or contact: Claims Conference Hardship Fund, 15 East 26th St., Room 906, New York, NY 10010; 212-696-4944.

E-mail: info@claimscon.org

Teachers and Police Officers Get 50 Percent Off!

That's one heck of a deal for a HUD house. Two programs from HUD, Officer Next Door and Teacher Next Door, are intended to strengthen revitalization areas by having police officers and teachers move into those neighborhoods.

Here's the money-saving low-down:

• Full-time employment by a federal, state, county, or municipal government or public or private educational agency is required.

• Teachers must be state-certified in grades K-12 and employed in the

---

Need Some Rent Assistance?

HUD has three programs that might help:

• Public housing: Low-income housing operated by your local housing authority.

• Section 8 vouchers: You can rent your own place, and the vouchers pay some, or all, of the rent.

• Privately owned subsidized housing: You rent it, and the government makes direct payment to the owner.

For more information, check the Federal Government section of your phone book for HUD.

---

school district in which the home they purchase is located.

• Police officers and teachers must reside in the home for a minimum of three years after purchase.

For more information, contact your local HUD office. View a listing of available HUD homes on the Web at www.hud.gov/tnd or www. hud.gov/ond/ond.html.

Who Will Buy Your Home and Then Let You Live in It Free?

Uncle Sam will, and his program, sponsored through HUD, is called reverse mortgage. Here's how it works:

• You must be 62 or older.

• You need to have a very low outstanding mortgage or own your home free and clear.

• You'll convert that equity into cash with a federally insured private loan.

• Repayment isn't required as long as the home is your principal residence.

And, here's the upside:

• No debt from a reverse mortgage will be passed to the estate or your heirs.

• You can't be forced to sell your home if the value decreases to a point that falls below the loan amount.

Want to find out more? Call 1-800-217-6970 or go to www.hud.gov/buying/rmtopten.cfm.

Going to the Country?

If small-town living is the life for you, then the Rural Housing Service might just have the housing assistance program you need. Here's what they offer:

• Single family home: Low-cost housing loans and grants go to low- and moderate-income rural families.

• Direct loan program: Loans go to those who can't qualify for a conventional loan.

• Self-help housing: Put in some labor, or "sweat equity," and knock off some of the cost.

• Home repair grants: These are targeted to people 62 or over.

• Rental Assistance Program: This provides that those in need will pay no more than 30 percent of their income for housing.

For more information, or to see if your brand of country living qualifies for a little help, go to www.rurdev.usda.gov, or contact: Rural Housing Service National Office, U.S. Department of Agriculture, Room 5037, South Building, 14th Street and Independence Ave. SW, Washington, DC 20250; 202-720-4323.

Money From HOME

It spills out of Uncle Sam's pockets right into your state's coffers, then it dribbles on down to local not-for-profit groups that rehabilitate and build affordable housing. But that's not all HOME money is good for. Here are some ways you can spend it:
• rental assistance
• rehabilitation of an existing house
• purchasing a home

There are financial limitations placed on HOME beneficiaries that vary according to location and change yearly. For more information, or to find out if you qualify, contact your local HUD office or write to: Office of Affordable Housing Programs, Office of Community Planning and Development, 451 7th Street SW, Washington, DC 20410, or visit the Web site at www.hud.gov/cpd/home/homeweb.html.

And Away You Go

Want to spend some time away, with all expenses paid? All you have to do is donate your expertise to the United Nations. Here are the programs for which you can volunteer:

• International Specialists serve in humanitarian relief, peace-building, and human rights programs.

• International Field Workers serve in education and self-help programs.

• National Specialists work at home with local governments and organizations.

• National Field Workers assist local self-help groups.

• UNISTAR volunteers are executives and technical experts who assist entrepreneurship in developing countries.

• TOTKEN volunteers are expatriates who return home to assist academic needs or research.

For more information on these programs, visit www.unv.org or write to: United Nations Volunteers, Postfach 260 111, D-53153 Bonn, Germany.

Another Free Trip

See Europe, the Near East, Asia, and Africa all courtesy of Uncle Sam. All you have to do is become a participant in the Professional Exchange Program, where you will share your skills with countries that need your expertise, and the trip could be yours. Here are some of the subject areas that have been recruited:

- conflict resolution
- environmental protection
- education administration
- media development
- judicial training
- small business development

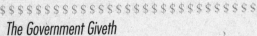

For more information, contact: Office of Citizen Exchanges, Bureau of Educational and Cultural Affairs, U.S. Department of State, SA-44, 301 Fourth St. SW, Washington, DC 20547; 202-619-5348.

Still More Travel

Hey artists! Here's your chance to get in on some Uncle Sam travel. The Cultural Programs Division of the State Department's Bureau of Educational and Cultural Affairs is looking for artists, filmmakers, and musicians who can demonstrate American diversity and creativity to foreign audiences. Areas being recruited are:

- literature programs
- cultural preservation instruction
- arts appreciation as an aid to promote social awareness
- artistic presentations that showcase the achievement of arts in America
- activities that promote the role of culture in economic development

For more information, contact: Cultural Programs Division Staff, Bureau of Educational and Cultural Affairs, U.S. Department of State, SA-44, 301 Fourth St. SW, Suite 568, Washington, DC 20547; 202-619-4779.

Chapter 4

Cyber Money Smarts

It's a risky proposition, going online with your money, but everybody's doing it. If you know what you're doing, cyber money matters can be incredibly convenient. But if you don't, you might see your dollars and cents being sucked away right through the monitor.

A Deal You Can't Beat!

How would you like to learn to use some of the most popular programs around? There are over 200 free training courses at freeskills.efront.com. You'll get to learn:

- courses on financial packages
- Microsoft
- Lotus
- Corel
- Novell
- Web development
- desktop publishing
- Internet tools
- databases
- desktop graphics

Go for it! You'll learn new computer skills or improve the skills you already have. The more you know, the safer your online journeys will be.

Hush, Hush!

That's how you should keep all your private information until you're sure who's on the other end of your mouse click. Here's how:

- Read the Web site privacy policy.

- Ask yourself these commonsense questions:

    —What information will be collected?

    —Is this info necessary for the transaction I'm considering?

    —Will the info be available to others?

    —Can I refuse to provide the info?

An important consideration for interacting with different Web sites is whether or not the site uses cookies. A cookie is a file from a Web site that attaches to your computer's hard drive. It can track your use of the site and tell the site a lot about your online habits.

For Your Own Financial Good

If you're going to participate in any kind of online financial adventure:

- Never use your Social Security number as an identifier.

Fast Fact

Do you need to secure your e-mail, with proof of delivery? The U.S. Post Office can do it for you. Visit the Web site at www. framed.usps.com/postecs.

- Keep your password to yourself, and change it periodically. The more complicated it is, such as a combination of random numbers and letters, the harder it is to crack.

- Where money or credit card transactions are concerned, deal only with a secure site. You'll know them by a tiny padlock or other secure symbol on the site. *Never, ever enter into a financial transaction on an unsecured site!*

- Consider buying software that will secure your

personal and financial information.

And If They Do Get the Private Goods

Breached online privacy is a cyberthief's paradise. Here's what a cyberthief can do:

• Open up a new credit card, leaving you with the bills.

• Charge up a storm on your credit cards. They'll even change your mailing address to misdirect the bills, then shop a little longer.

• Set up a cellular phone account. They call, you pay.

• Open a bank account in your name, then bounce, bounce, bounce checks, also in your name.

Unfortunately, getting your personal information can

be as easy as sending you an e-mail that looks like it's from your Internet Service Provider, stating that your account needs to be updated. If you're not paying attention, you might easily respond, providing the cyberthieves with all they need to know on a silver platter.

Making Those Online Payments

The easiest way to pay for something is always just to hand over the green stuff, but that's not an online option. Here are a few ways you can cyber pay:

• Use your credit card! *This is the safest online payment method.* You have recourse, through your credit card company, to contest payment for fraudulent, misrepre-

---

Fast Fact

Already a cyber privacy victim? Call the Federal Trade Commission at their toll-free Identity Theft Hotline, 877-IDTHEFT, or go online to www.consumer.gov/idtheft and make your report.

---

sented, or otherwise bad services or products.

• Debit cards allow quick payment, dipping directly into your account almost immediately. But consider if you really want someone else's hands in your pot.

• You can always send a check through the mail.

• A payment account allows the entire transaction to take place online. You issue the go-ahead, and a payment company makes the payment. For more info on this, go to www.PayPal.com.

The New Kid on the Block

It's electronic money, in the form of a stored-value card. Similar to a phone card, you buy it for a certain cash value, and it is debited when you make an online purchase. The big advantage is that you don't have to give out personal information, but there are disadvantages:

• You may not be covered for theft or loss.

• The card may have an expiration date.

Many companies and financial institutions offer stored-value cards. Check with your banker for more information.

Cybershopping

It's easy and so much fun. You don't even have to get out of your jammies to do it. But make sure you cybershop the right way so you're protected.

• Shop with companies you know. If you don't know a company, request a paper catalog before you buy online.

• Make sure the return and refund policy and the shipping charges are OK with you.

• Print a copy of your order and confirmation number.

Frenzy!

This is what happens at the online auction when worldwide buyers click in at lightning speed to bid on that black velvet painting of Elvis. If you really want him hanging in your home, here are some buying safety tips:

• Check the seller's feedback rating from previous buyers.

• Contact the seller and ask questions; ask about the return policy.

• Don't bid if the seller won't accept returns.

• Don't bid if the seller hasn't included a picture in the description of the item.

• If you buy an item you think was misrepresented, try to work it out with the seller. Legitimate sellers don't want bad feedback. If you can't come to terms, contact the auction company.

Here's Where the Big Money Goes!

Online auctions are great for the antiques dealer—

Foreign Cyber

If shipping and handling charges are far more than you expected, you could be dealing with a company outside the country. Inside the United States, you have rights as a consumer, but these may not apply to foreign transactions.

Make sure you know:
• *if dollars are posted in U.S. currency*
• *if there are additional import duties or taxes*
• *where you can go to resolve a problem*

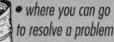

Money $ecrets

low overhead costs. But they come with some warnings for the casual buyer— did you know that *a full one-fourth of all sales are misrepresented*? So before you fork over a fortune to buy your heart's desire, follow all the above auction advice, plus:

• Run to the library, consult a price guide, and set your limit.

• Beware of qualifying terms—*looks* Victorian, Victorian *appearance,* Victorian*like.*

• Know your condition terminology:

—These are bad: *worn, fair, average, some wear.*

—These are good: *very good, nice, choice, excellent, mint, mint in box.*

• Regardless of what the description claims, ask the seller about condition; are there any dings, chips, rust spots, repairs, restorations, cracks, or other flaws?

Even in E-mail

Ten thousand people have become rich after they passed this letter along to others. Just send $1.00 to each of the top ten names, forward this to 500 e-mail friends, and wait until your name hits the top. Yeah, just like Florida swampland is a good investment, too.

• Chain letters that ask for money or anything else of value are illegal, regardless of the form in which they arrive.

• If you pass along a chain letter of this sort, you're breaking the law.

• If you decide to send one of these letters anyway, don't hold your breath waiting to receive your payoff.

For more information, contact your local U.S. Postal Inspection Service office.

You Can't Run Away

Electronic banking is here to stay, in the form of:

- automated teller machines
- direct deposit
- pay-by-phone
- online banking

We're familiar with the first three, but number four is still a little intimidating. It has advantages, though. You can:

- view your account balance online
- request transfers between accounts
- pay bills

Everything about your banking life is tied up in a computer anyway, so if you think online banking could be convenient:

- See if your bank offers the service; most major banks do.

- Make sure your bank's insured through the FDIC. You can verify that fact at www.fdic.gov/bank.

Electronic Funds Transfers

You know them—the payments deducted from your account every month. You set them up and the computer does the rest. But those computers can make mistakes and accidentally pay your insurance bill six times in a month.

Before you set up an EFT account, ask your institution to provide the following information in written form:

- a summary of your liability for unauthorized transfers
- contact information to report errors
- fees for transfer
- frequency and dollar limits
- your right to:
    —receive transfer documentation
    —stop payments on preauthorized transfers
- the institution's liability if it fails to make or stop certain payments

Net Loss

Online investment opportunities abound. Many are legitimate, but some are not. How can you tell the difference?

- First, use your head. If it sounds too good to be true, it is.

- Don't fall for the line: "This investment is IRA approved." It's a lie—the government does not approve investments for IRAs.

Your Computer's Overseas Buddy

This one can really cost you big, big bucks in a short, short time!

- You download a program that offers free international calls.

- It disconnects your Internet connection and reconnects to an international long-distance number. The calls may be free, but the connection is not. It can cost you up to $7 per minute.

Here's what you can do if you get stuck in one of these programs:

- Beware of any program that enables your modem to redial to the Internet.

- If you see that it's dialing when you don't want it to, cancel the connection.

- Read the disclosure language. To stay legal, these services often do tell you what they're doing, but it's in the microscopic print.

- If it happens to you, call the FTC at 877-FTC-HELP.

- Save your phone bill for proof.

Fast Fact

Online trading—it's easy, convenient, and oftentimes inexpensive. And if you know your stuff, you can probably take advantage of those benefits. But don't be suckered in by the ads if you're not a regular trader. Online trading is for the stock-market literate only, and you could lose your initial investment, your fees, and your shirt if you are stock-market impaired.

Chapter 5

Supermarket Savvy

You walk through their doors 2.3 times a week to spend $87 for your family, making your selections from almost 50,000 items. Imagine if you could cut your spending by 10 percent. The savings would give you about five weeks' worth of free groceries. These tips can help you achieve some of those savings.

Buy Me! Buy Me!

The products might as well be screaming this as you walk through the door. Have you ever noticed how the pretzels are so conveniently sitting right next to the beer? It's called integrated marketing, and that translates to impulse buying, which coaxes you into spending up to 50 percent more than you'd planned. Here are some ways your grocer induces you to buy those un-planned extras:

- aroma from the bakery
- free samples
- announcements
- placement of holiday merchandise everywhere
- pop-up coupon dis-pensers
- checkout area lined with as much stuff as will squeeze in

But how can you handle your impulse to buy? Here are some ways:

- Plan for one or two impulse items.

- Set a small impulse budget; about 10 percent of your overall purchases.

- Don't go to the checkout immediately. You might have second thoughts.

Shelving Their Way Into Your Wallet

Your grocer has a big secret. The way the aisles and shelves are set up is meant to get you to dig deeper into your pockets. Here are some of the top money-grabbing shelf tricks of the grocery trade.

- Highest-priced items are at eye level.

- Displays at the aisle ends may look like they're on sale, but many really aren't.

- Kids' foods are placed at their eye level.

- Shelves are rearranged often to make shoppers find new products when searching for their regulars.

- Food sections are scattered so you'll hunt: Half the crackers may be on one side of the store, and half on the other.

- Store brands are placed among corresponding name brands; the pricing sign highlights savings, but the grocer's real motivation is that store brands reap higher profits for the grocer.

- Older food products are shifted to the front of the shelf to sell before their expiration date. If you want the freshest possible food, check toward the back of the stack.

Fast Fact

Why is the milk always at the back of the store? Because everyone buys it, and the hike to find it will take us past most of those other 50,000 items in the store.

Read Between the Lines

Yes, grocery stores have their own lingo. Understanding it can add up to big savings.

• *Two-for-one sale:* Be careful. Regular prices may have been hiked substantially to offset the sale.

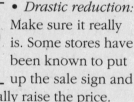

• *Loss leader:* These products lure you into the store with their unbelievably low prices, and the store will actually lose money on them. Their hope is that you'll buy more once you get inside.

• *Conditional bargains:* "No rain checks" or "With a $10 purchase." Like loss leaders, these can be the greatest bargain you'll find, but read the conditions in the fine print. The store could put a limiting condition on the deal.

• *Drastic reduction:* Make sure it really is. Some stores have been known to put up the sale sign and actually raise the price.

Color Conditioning Can Cost You

Package designers grab your attention by taking advantage of your emotional response to colors. Here's what they know about your subconscious impulses that causes you to fork over extra bucks:

More Color Conditioning

Yes, you are conditioned to respond to color ads and store signs. Traditionally, red has always meant bargain or sale. Consequently, many advertisers use red to draw your attention, then lure you into believing you're getting a great deal. But watch out. The deal you're conditioned to seeing in the color red may not be a sale at all.

- Buying red packaging or product names in bold print makes people think they're buying power.

- Yellow is the most visible color on the shelf. It makes shoppers think they see larger packages, even though they don't. It also reminds consumers of sun and warmth.

- When customers see blue packages, they tend to think of serenity, confidence, wisdom, purity, and cleanliness.

- Green brings to mind natural, environmentally safe, healthy qualities.

- Buying white invokes feelings of freshness.

- Consumers feel elegant and sophisticated when they buy black packaging.

Some Costly Tricks of the Trade

You're on their turf, playing their game, but that doesn't mean they have to win. Here are three ways you can take home the savings trophy.

- Love that cheese? Count how many places it's sold in your store. Always two, and sometimes three. Compare prices for the same product in different areas—they won't be the same. And it's a sure bet deli-sliced cheddar will cost you more than cheddar that's already packaged.

- Hungry? When you walk in the store you'll probably be accosted by the smell of freshly fried chicken or baked goods. Store-cooked foods are up front for a reason—to remind you that you're hungry, because when you're hungry, you buy more groceries. So don't go to the store hungry.

- Want convenience? You're paying a lot for it.

Most convenience foods are only a few ingredients, so you can easily make your own. Look on the Web for recipes to create your own products similar to Shake 'n Bake, Rice-a-Roni, and many others at busycooks.about.com. Spend an afternoon putting it all together, and you'll have enough for months.

Other Food Business Tricks

Shrinking content weight hides a price increase. It's perfectly legal, and it's a sneaky trick that works. The packaging changes imperceptibly so that the buyer cannot tell he or she is getting less product, but the price stays the same. Here are some downsizing tricks:

• changing the way biscuits are arranged inside plastic packaging to reduce the number of biscuits that fit into the new configuration

• reducing the number of sheets on a toilet roll or roll of paper towels

• changing the shape of a bottle so that it appears to be larger than other products with the same volume

• keeping the height of a bottle or can the same but reducing its diameter

Take This Shopping to Another Store

Nonfood items in a grocery store fall into the category of "gotcha!" They will usually get you in the wallet because they are high markup items that compensate for loss leaders and other bargains. But it's easier for you to buy your toilet paper at the grocery store than to traipse to a discount store, and guess who knows that? So traipse, and save money when you stock up on these things:

- toilet paper
- paper towels and napkins
- shampoo
- tissue
- toothpaste
- trash bags
- cosmetics
- laundry and dish detergent
- pet foods and supplies

Shop at Bag-It-Yourself Stores

Shop at the bag-it-yourself stores at least once a month to stock up on staples. The prices cannot be beat, though you may not find those specialty brands. If you absolutely have to have them, shop here first for everything you can, and bring your own bags. Then go to the regular store.

Shop at Farmers' Markets

Shop early and get the cream of the crop, or go later and get the best buys. Prices on fruits, vegetables, and flowers don't get much lower. And you'd be hard pressed to find food much fresher than direct from the farm.

Shop at Thrift Bakery Stores

Get day-old bread and baked goods for about half the cost of what's in the grocery store. But be sure to buy only as many perishables as you can easily store and use. There's certainly no point in saving money on day-old pastries if you're not going to be able to serve or eat them all.

Pick Your Day

Remember the last time you tried to grab a bag of frozen green beans but had to wait in the aisle behind three other people who were comparing prices, reading nutritional labels, or just studying the picture? Next time, plan your shopping day based on this list, in order from the least shopped days of the week to the most:

- Wednesday
- Sunday
- Friday
- Tuesday and Thursday
- Monday
- Saturday

And be sure to avoid these shopping times:

- the day before a holiday
- Labor Day or Memorial Day weekend
- July 4th
- the days before and after Thanksgiving
- the day after a natural disaster
- when impending bad weather (blizzard, hurricane) is announced
- any day between 4 and 7 P.M.

Do They Love You?

Of course grocery stores love you, and they'll give you special discounts to prove it. In the industry

Should You Sign Up?

You can make a pretty good grocery killing with preferred-shopper programs, but when you fill out a membership application, remember that you're being tracked. If privacy is important to you, here are some questions you should ask before signing up:

- Will this information be sold or transferred?

- Can you stop that sale or transfer?

- How is this information used?

- Can your name and information be removed from the database?

this is called *loyalty marketing*, but you've probably seen it yourself as a preferred-shopper program. For your loyalty, you can get some great buys. Here are the most common programs:

• Frequent-shopper: You'll be issued a free card that the store will use to track your shopping habits and award you points based on the dollar amounts you spend. Accumulated points, like frequent flyer miles, can be exchanged for discounts or cash off on purchases.

• Purchase-triggered coupons: When you buy targeted products, you'll receive a store coupon for a competing brand or dollars off on your next shopping trip.

• Instant discounts: A cashier will scan your membership card, and you'll reap the benefit of a "members only" sale.

Two More Costly Tricks of the Trade

There are even more ways they can get you. Here are a couple:

• "Limit 4 per customer." This implies a good deal, but what it really does is induce many customers to buy the item because they *think* it's a good deal. Many times it isn't, but the limit imposed causes some customers to go for more than they would normally.

• Don't be tempted by time-consuming frills such as a café or video rental. The longer you spend in a grocery store, the more money you'll spend. And they know it. Thirty minutes is as long as you should ever need to stay in their establishment, because for every minute you stay over that you'll spend 50 cents.

Want to Save Hundreds of $$$?

Use coupons. If you're good at it, you can save 15 percent of your total grocery bill. Here's how:

• Collect them from wherever you find them: newspapers, magazines, mailbox ads, and in-store displays.

• Don't waste time with coupons for products you don't use, even if you think you might use them someday. This tempts you to buy something you wouldn't normally spend money on.

• Combine offers. Use your coupons when the item is on sale or when a rebate is offered with it.

• Check the in-store flyer for other specials such as *get a free gallon of milk with a $10 purchase and this coupon.*

• Arrange your coupon file to match the order that the products appear as you stroll through the store. Use a clothespin or large clip to attach the coupons to your cart as you select items.

Turn Your Computer Into a Coupon Factory

That's right. At www. valupage.com, you can make your own coupons. Follow the instructions, choose the products that interest you, print the page, and take it to your local merchant. After you buy the products you selected at the Web site, the store will print out coupons in the form of Web Bucks, which you can use toward your next grocery purchases (whether

___

Fast Fact

Over 400 billion coupons are issued every year; over 95 percent of them are never used.

___

you buy those same items again or not). At the Web site, just click on the specials you want and print out a page to take along shopping so you can buy the products that earn the savings coupons.

And Don't Forget the Rebates

Studies show that only about 5 percent of all shoppers make good on rebates all the time. And that's exactly what the companies offering the rebates are counting on. They can offer the low rebated sale price, but the odds of your asking for that money back are slim. So they're the finder and you're the loser.

The points against using the rebate:
- too much effort
- cost of postage
- takes too long to collect

But there's one big reason for you to use rebates:

Dollar amounts are higher than coupons. Look in these places to find your rebate slips:
- store customer service desk or bulletin board
- the display or package itself
- toll-free number listed on the package to call the manufacturer directly

Do the List

Even though 80 percent of the things you buy this week will be the same as what you buy next week or what you bought last week, don't let that lull you into the I can shop without a list mode. Without your list, you'll find yourself running through the aisles, buying everything your grocer really wants to sell you. Make the list. It will save you up to 50 percent off your willy-nilly spree.

List-Making Time-Saver

Create an all-purpose grocery list on your computer, and make photocopies you can grab before you shop. Glance over the list, highlight the things you need, and you'll be armed for bargain-hunting. You can download a generic list from www.geocities.com/ akimbopress/books.html.

Credits Cards Save Money? You've Got to Be Kidding!

Studies show that almost three-fourths of people who use credits cards to shop for groceries pay off their balance at the end of each month. This means they have no finance charge. So if you don't carry a balance, go for it. These are the advantages you can reap:

• credit card bonus programs: frequent flier miles, cash back bonus

• ability to stock up on unexpected sales

The Big Battle: Name Brand vs. Generic

A lot of what you buy depends on the way things taste to you. If you're strictly a brand-name shopper, you probably spend up to 40 percent more than you need to. Here's a name brand vs. generic list of items that are the same, regardless of the label they wear. Start with these, and maybe you'll add a few more store brands on your own.

• baking soda
• cooking oil (except olive)
• cornstarch
• extracts and flavorings
• herbs
• lemon and lime juice
• salt
• spices
• sugar
• unbleached flour
• vinegar

Read the Fine Print

The unit price is the fine print on the shelf price tag, and it can save you several cents per purchase. The unit price tells you what you're paying per ounce, and it's the best way to compare brands or sizes. (Hint: A common misconception is that buying in bulk is the cheapest, but that's often not the case. You've got to read the unit price to find out.)

Scanner Secrets

The first biggie is that scanners are not always accurate. Now here are a few more:

• You're charged the wrong price about 3.5 percent of the time; overcharged 2 percent and undercharged 1.5 percent.

• Sales items cause the majority of errors. They're charged incorrectly up to 10 percent of the time.

• Scanner overcharges are more likely to occur on the first day of a sale.

Now that you know, here's what can you do.

• Watch the scanning total carefully.

• Keep sales ads with you for handy checkout reference.

• Write down all sale prices.

• Ask the cashier to send someone to check out a price.

And here's the supersaver tip of the day: Ask if the store has a policy to give you, free, any items that scan for more than the sticker or shelf label price. Many do, but they don't advertise the fact.

Fast Fact

Why do store brands cost so much less? They don't have the huge advertising budgets name-brand products do.

Chapter 6

Buyer Beware!

One of the biggest money-saving secrets you'll ever hear is, "Don't spend it if you don't know what you're getting in return." New ways for scammers to get their hands into your pockets come up daily. Here are some of their best tricks to take your hard-earned money.

Make $10,000 a Month From Home

Yeah, right. If it could be done, everyone would be doing it. Here are the most common work-at-home schemes that will do nothing but work your money into their greedy hands.

• Envelope stuffing: "For a *small fee*, learn how to make big bucks." If you send that fee, guess what you'll get in return. Nothing but a letter inviting you to join the scam by placing that same envelope-stuffing ad in more magazines and newspapers.

• Assembly (or craft) work at home: You buy the supplies and production equipment from them, and they'll buy back the finished product. But the catch is that nothing you'll ever create will meet their "standards," and they won't buy back a single thing.

Getting Help

If you're a victim of any scam involving financial or property loss:

• Report it to the attorney general in both your state and the state in which the company is located, if you know where that is.

• Contact your local consumer protection office, Better Business Bureau, and/or postmaster (if it involved anything to do with the U.S. mail).

• Explain your story to the advertising manager of the publication that ran the ad.

• Call the Federal Trade Commission complaint line at 877-FTC-HELP, or fill out the online complaint form at www.ftc.gov.

There are no guarantees that you'll recover what you lost, but the more people you alert, the better your chances—and the safer other consumers will be.

Congratulations! It's Your Lucky Day!

You've won a Hawaiian vacation, grandfather clock, or $5,000 cash. And here's all you have to do to claim one of the prizes:

• Sit through a hard-pitch sales presentation.

• Ante up a big-time shipping fee.

But for one of those great prizes, isn't it worth it? If you'd love a four-inch plastic grandfather clock replica, the answer's yes. And that's what you'll get—the one clinker sandwiched between the two great prizes.

Bottom line: Don't fall for the prize-winning call or postcard. *And never return a call to inquire.* You could be dialing into an area code where the real scam is what you're paying by the minute.

Newly Approved Slave Reparations

This scam is springing to life in African American communities. The flyers magically appear in senior citizens centers, churches, and nursing homes, and they claim that:

• African Americans born before 1928 may be eligible for slave reparations.

• Those born from 1917 to 1926 can apply to Social Security for funds due to a "fix" in the system.

No way! Slave reparations don't exist. What's really happening is that swindlers are trying to get your personal information. Contact the Federal Trade Commission Identity Theft Hotline at 877-IDTHEFT for more information.

Please Let Me Help You

For a small fee, Madam Scam will get you through the Social Security red tape by helping you:
• apply for benefits
• apply for disability benefits
• apply for a new or replacement card

Same Scam, Different Verse

They also want to get their hands on your personal information if you were born from 1911 to 1926 (called a "Notch Baby"). To get a "Notch Baby" Social Security "settlement," you must supply your name, date of birth, and Social Security number to something called National Victim's Register. They'll give you an official Washington, D.C., address, but don't give any information back. It's a fraud, too.

- change your address
- get information about a deceased family member
- change your name
- request a statement of earnings and benefits

Hogwash! You don't need to pay to get those Social Security chores done because you can do them yourself for free. Go to www.ssa.gov to see how easy it is.

Beggars and Thieves

Charities collect $143 billion a year, of which 10 percent ends up in the pockets of swindlers. Before you give, ask for:
- written information verifying the charity's name, address, and phone number
- personal identification

Then:

- Don't trust the letterhead. Instead, call the charity.

- Don't give in to pressure tactics.

- Don't give out credit card information.

- Before you do anything, contact one of these for verification:
—American Institute of Philanthropy at 301-913-5200, www.charitywatch.org
—National Charities Information Bureau at 212-929-6300, www.give.org

Petal Pushers

Yes, even the florist might be ripping you off. Here's how:

- She places an ad in your local phone directory

using your town name so you'll think it's a local business.

• You phone an order to this out-of-towner and pay by credit card.

Telemarketing Savvy

Don't be out-slicked by the phone slicker. Here are some ways to deal with him:

• Don't buy from an unfamiliar company.

• Ask him to send you written information.

• Check his information with the local consumer protection agency or Better Business Bureau.

• Never make a snap decision.

• Do not give out your credit card or bank account information.

• If you think it's a scam, just hang up.

• She transfers the order to your local florist.

• She gets a cut from the sale plus a processing fee, which you pay for.

To make sure you aren't dealing with someone across the country:

• Deal only with shops listing a street address.

• Ask for directions to the shop. If she hesitates or refuses to say, hang up.

Ring-a-Ding-Ding

They're calling to rip you off. If the caller on the other end of the line wants your money for *anything*, be cautious. Here are some things you'll hear from the phonies:

• "You must act now. This offer won't be good after this phone call!"

• "We need your credit card or bank account number."

• "This is a no-risk offer."

Every year, 14,000 illegal telemarketing operations grab up $40 billion. Make sure your dollars aren't counted among that total.

Don't Double Your Trouble

So you bought something from a telemarketer and got cheated. Once is bad enough, so don't do it again. Here's what can happen:

• Your name goes on a "sucker" list.

• Another scammer buys the list to find out who to trick again.

• The new scammer calls you, offering to recover the money you lost from the first scam—for a fee.

Some legitimate organizations do try to help you recover your money, but they don't charge fees or make guarantees. If you've been scammed and perhaps scammed again, call the National Fraud Information Center at 800-876-7060 for more information.

Fee Fi Foe Fum

These fees really are your foe:

• "We guarantee you'll get that loan as soon as you pay us an application fee!" Don't believe it. Advance-fee loans are a scam. Legitimate lending institutions never guarantee, and they don't require any application fees.

• "For a fee, learn how to get unlimited profits exchanging money on world currency markets! This is the secret to making $4,000 in one day." If that were true, everyone would be rich, wouldn't they?

• "We'll erase negative credit information from your file for a fee." No way. Legitimate credit counseling agencies deal in debt repayment, not vanishing acts.

The Lowdown on Infomercials

It looks like a TV show, sounds like one, and probably features a celebrity. But watch out!

• The product could cost much less in a local store.

• Shipping and handling terms could be exorbitant.

• Celebrities earn money for endorsements, so it's only an acting job to them.

• For noncelebrity testimonials, it's a paid job or a chance to get on camera.

If you're still interested:

• Shop around in local stores first.

• Don't be taken in by slashed payments or free gifts if you *order in the next 10 minutes*. You'll get the same deal no matter when you order.

This Pyramid Isn't in Egypt

You recruit someone and they recruit someone else. And you make money down the line, from anyone who was recruited by someone you recruited. Got it? Well, if you don't, they'll get *you*. Here's how to spot a pyramid scheme coming at you:

• Products are sold to other distributors, not to the public.

• The terms used are "multilevel" or "network" marketing.

• The claim is that your big money will come from those you recruit, not your sales.

Pyramid schemes come in every form, but the one thing they all have in common is that you have to pay up to join up. Do your homework. Check with the Better Business Bureau first.

Chapter 7

Energy Saved Means Money in Your Pocket

Wow! With rising energy prices, you can't afford one little leak or draft in your house. Energy inefficiency means wasted money, and unless you have money to burn, you'd better read on to save hundreds of $$$ a year.

Before You Go Further!

Your house isn't 100-percent energy efficient. No house is. But how can you find out where the problems are and how to solve them? Just take this free home-energy audit.

• Go to hit.lbl.gov for the Home Improvement Tool.

• Answer a few questions about your home's structure, heating and cooling, and appliances.

• Add up your various annual energy bills either separately or lumped together for one total.

• Wait for an analysis of your five biggest energy-losing problems as well as advice on how to fix them.

Stargazing

It doesn't take a telescope to find an ENERGY STAR. The Environmental Protection Agency and Department of Energy have hitched them to 3,400 highly efficient, money-saving, planet-saving home products. So, to cut a whopping 30 percent off your yearly energy bills, look for this label when you replace old products.

Cool It

When you turn on the air conditioner and bask in the cool, you're doubling your electric bill. On very hot days it's probably worth the price, but you can still save a little money while staying cool.

• Reduce the use of heat generating sources: ovens, dishwashers, and dryers.

• Turn off the lights.

• Switch to fluorescent bulbs, which use 73 percent less energy than regular bulbs and emit 90 percent less heat.

• Paint your walls white. White walls absorb less heat than dark walls.

Oh, Those Naughty Windows

They can draw in 40 percent of the unwanted heat in your house during the summer, and they're responsible for up to 25 percent of your winter heating bill. But don't despair. Here are some low-cost seasonal tips.

During winter:

• Install tight-fitting, insulating window shades.

• Keep shades and curtains closed at night and open during the day.

During summer:

• Use white window shades, drapes, and blinds to reflect heat away from the house.

• During the day, close drapes and blinds on the south and west windows. Install awnings on these windows, as well.

Air-Conditioning Savers

Your unit should have the right cooling capacity for your space. Anything too large wastes energy and money.

• To figure out what the right capacity is, go to the Association of Home Appliances Manufacturers estimate form at www. aham.org/consumer/ getstartcoolload.htm.

• Don't restrict airflow in or out of the unit.

• Put the unit on the east or north side of the house.

• Set the thermostat to as warm as you can tolerate.

Whistles and Bells on Your Fridge

They're fun, but they're oh so expensive. These are some of the more notorious energy eaters:

Facing Facts

Windows don't live forever. Many people think that selecting replacements is tough, but nowadays it's actually pretty simple. Here are some facts you should remember:

• In colder climates, buy windows with low emissivity (low-e) coatings. They reduce heat loss by radiating heat from the infrared waves, which is the portion of sunlight that warms your house. This means they grab the heat and direct it inside.

• In warmer climates, buy windows with spectrally selective coatings. They block the infrared rays. In other words, the sun shines in, but the heat's blocked out.

- in-door water and ice dispensers
- inside-freezer ice makers
- side-by-side models, which consume 35 percent more energy than freezer-on-top models
- models with anti-sweat heaters, which consume 10 percent more energy than those with automatic moisture controls

When to Set Sale

There's a time and season for every appliance sale: after Easter, after July 4th, after Christmas. Before starting the hunt, check out these appliance bargain-buying months.

- January
  —freezers
  —ranges
  —refrigerators
- February
  —air conditioners
  —ranges
- March
  —air conditioners
  —ranges
- June
  —freezers
  —refrigerators
- August
  —air conditioners

Extended Warranty, Yes or No?

Be very careful before you make the commitment. You could be spending unnecessary bucks to add coverage already included in the one-year manufacturer's warranty that comes with the appliance. Ask about the manufacturer's warranty before you plunk down your dollars, and also ask if you can purchase an extended warranty at the end of the first year. Some salespeople will say yes, but many will say no, which is usually a pressure tactic. Don't believe them. You'll probably receive an extended warranty offer before you and your appliance celebrate your first anniversary together.

- September
  —air conditioners
- November
  —ranges

Guess What Doesn't Go on Vacation

When you leave home, did you know that all the little energy guzzlers you left behind throw a party at your expense? Here are some energy-saving suggestions.

- Empty your refrigerator and set it at the warmest possible temperature. This saves energy by 40 percent.

- Shut down the water heater. Unplug the instant-hot-water device on your faucet, too.

- Put your inside lights on a timer and your outside lights on a motion sensor. This saves energy use by 80 percent.

Fast Fact

Whenever you appliance shop, make sure you're getting the best buy for your money. Check ratings in *Consumer Guide*, which is available from most magazine retailers and in libraries.

- Unplug constantly running appliances such as clocks and cordless phones.

It All Comes Out in the Wash

Well, at least $200 a year can, if you make a few changes in your laundry habits. Since 90 percent of the cost of washing your clothes is tied up in the hot water, here are a few ways to untie that cost.

- Rinse in cold water. The rinse cycle has nothing to do with getting your clothes clean.

- If you use hot water, match the water level to the load size.

- Wash clothes that are not too soiled in warm or cold water. Some detergents are made specifically for cold-water washing.

• Don't overuse detergent. Getting too sudsy makes your machine work harder and gobble up more energy.

One Big Water Heater Guzzler

This baby is your third biggest energy-eater, claiming at least 14 percent of your utility bill. Consider this: A family of four, each showering five minutes a day, uses 700 gallons of water per week. You can cut that in half with low-flow, nonaerating showerheads. Now, here are some other energy-saving hot-water tips.

• Place an insulation jacket around the water heater.

• Lower your water-heater thermostat to 115 degrees.

• Drain a quart of water from your heater every three months to get rid of sediment that impedes heater efficiency.

• When you turn on the cold water, don't let your faucet handle venture into hot-water territory. It revs up the heater even if you don't want hot water.

Warming It Up

Staying warm costs big bucks, but these tips will help cut back on part of the cost without cutting back on the heat.

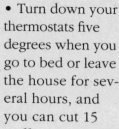

• Turn down your thermostats five degrees when you go to bed or leave the house for several hours, and you can cut 15 percent off your monthly heating bill.

• Change furnace filters once a month. The cleaner your furnace, the more efficiently it heats.

• Insulate your ductwork. If it's not insulated, you can be losing up to 40 percent of your furnace's output.

\$ \$

72   *Money \$ecrets*

Freebies From Your Utility Company

This list is pretty short, but you might as well grab some of this free stuff if your utility company offers it:

- flourescent bulbs
- water-heater jackets
- home energy audits to determine problem areas
- low-flow showerheads

Save Some Energy When You Cook

All the best chefs know these tips.

- Pressure cookers, slow cookers, and steamers are more efficient than range-top pans and ovens.

- Heating a small meal in a toaster oven uses half the energy you'd use in a regular oven.

- Frozen meats take 20 minutes per pound longer to cook than do thawed meats.

- Preheat the oven only for baked goods that require an exact starting temperature.

- Keep your burner reflectors clean. They reflect the heat up to the pan, which is where it should go.

- Keep foil off the bottom of the oven. It impairs heat circulation and drops the temperature up to 50 degrees.

All About Your Microwave

You know it's quick, but did you know these facts?

- For 85 percent of all your cooking tasks, a microwave will cut your energy cost by 50 percent.

- A microwave baking four potatoes uses 65 percent less energy than a regular oven.

On the downside, don't boil water or other liquids. To bring four cups of water to boil, a microwave will use 10 percent more energy than a pot on your rangetop.

Chapter 8

Credit, Debit, Banking, and Insurance Smarts

You squander a few bucks, and someone says, "There's more where that came from." That's fine if it's their money, but not if it's yours. You worked too hard to get it, and you have no intention of getting rid of it if you don't have to. So here are some tips for great ways to hang on to what's yours.

An Account's an Account, Right?

You've got checking choices, and they can be confusing. Here are some money-saving features to look for when you're opening your account.

- free checks: many banks will give them to seniors
- no per-check fee for each check you write
- free travelers checks
- interest payments
- free ATM transactions
- low-cost or nonexistent service fee

- free payment service for utilities
- free electronic funds transfer

Banks and other financial institutions won't just hand out these special offers when you walk in the door. You have to ask for them. In many cases, you may be required to maintain a minimum balance. But a little comparison shopping for your checking account can add up to a little extra cash in your checking account.

Everything's Negotiable

In a bank, nothing is as it appears if you put in your two cents worth for a better deal. So, negotiate any of these:
- everything you've already read in this chapter
- loan fees
- fees for debit cards
- notary services

Try your hand at negotiating interest rates as well. If another bank offers you a great rate, take it to your bank and ask them to do better. And don't forget the safe-deposit box in case

Minimum Balance Blues

Always ask how much you have to keep in your account to avoid a monthly service charge. Then ask how that minimum balance is calculated. If they tell you it's calculated by the lowest balance of the month, you'll get smacked with the monthly fee if your account dipped below the allowable line for just one day.

 If possible, find a bank that uses the average of your daily balances to figure the monthly minimum. That way, one little slipup probably won't cause the monthly fee to kick in.

you need to keep some valuables there. You may even be able to get one for free if you have several accounts at that bank.

Cheap! Cheap!

Banks will have you believe you must order your checks from them, but that's not true. Check out these facts:

• Bank checks are printed by independent printers, so you're paying for two profit cuts, the bank's and the printer's.

• Bank checks can cost $20 for a box of 200.

Now compare:

• Independent check printers sell directly to you, so there's only one profit cut.

• Independent check printers can sell you a box of 200 checks for $5 or $6, sometimes much less if you get in on a special.

To find the bargain check companies, look for their flyers in newspapers, mailers, and magazines.

Minimize Those ATM Fees

That money machine can be a costly little gadget. The banks will charge you coming and going. If you use an ATM from a bank other than your own, you can pay one charge to your bank and another to the bank that owns the ATM. Here are some ATM tips:

• Use the ATM at your own bank, where you'll probably get unlimited free transactions.

• Read the fee notices on the ATM screen.

Are You Paying to Insure Your Bank?

Insuring your money is one thing, but do you really want to pay for your bank, too? Here's how it happens.

• You get a loan.

• The bank takes out disability or life insurance

on that loan, often as part of the loan, and makes itself the beneficiary.

• You could be paying loan-rate interest on that insurance.

• They don't tell you about it and hope you won't read it in the teeny, tiny print.

Here's what you can do: Just say *no way* up front, before the negotiations begin.

Skip the Bank for These

No matter what they tell you, the bank is the wrong place to buy these:

• insurance
• stock
• mutual funds

Why? The bank acts as a go-between. Because the bank has to get its cut of the profit, your costs for the product will be higher.

Scamming the Debits

Yep. It's another way to steal your money. And this scam has long fingers that dip right down into your checking account. Here's how it works.

• You get a "free prize" phone call.

• The telemarketer asks: "Do you have a checking account?"

• You get the too-good-to-be-true pitch, plus "Just read me those numbers on the bottom of your check so I can get this thing going for you."

Bam! You've just given the telemarketer your account and bank routing numbers, which means he can route money out of your account into his.

The best advice (and you've heard it before) is: Don't give out your information. But if you do and it results in your getting scam-debited, call your bank immediately.

Bad Credit? No Credit? No Problem!

Just establish an account with a few hundred dollars as security, the ads tell you, and you'll get a "secured" credit card. But there are both bad and good cards.

Bad cards:

• Require you to call a "900" number for an application. You may pay $50 or more per call.

• Lead you to another "900" call.

There are also legitimate secured cards, but they come with a couple of warnings:

• higher annual fees and interest rates than regular cards

• processing and application fees

For a list of legitimate institutions offering secured cards, send a $4 check or money order to BankCard Holders of America at: Secured Credit Card List, BHA Customer Service, 524 Branch Drive, Salem, VA 24153.

Card Shopping for Bargains

Here are money-savers to think about while you're shopping for credit cards.

• If it's a bank-issued card, ask them to waive the annual fee.

• The interest rate is actually negotiable with the issuer.

• The grace period they give you before interest

Credit Check

Want a peek at your credit report? In some states it's free, but in others it costs about $8. Copies are available from:

• Equifax: 800-997-2493 or www.equifax.com
• Experian: 800-311-4769 or www.experian.com
• Trans Union: 800-493-2392 or www.truecredit.com

kicks in doesn't apply to cash advances. That interest starts immediately.

• Finance charges include not only the interest but other charges for transactions such as cash advances. Check the fine print.

• If you're late by a day, you can pay an extra $30. If your bank issues the card, find out if you can make a last-minute payment there to avoid the fine.

Chop That Insurance Premium in Half!

Then chop it in half again. It's easy! But the insurance people aren't telling you how to do it because they'd rather put the entire amount into their pockets instead of only 25 percent. Here's how you can get an individual policy for just a fraction of what they want to charge.

Fast Fact

Are you easy to insure? Then reinsure every few years. Initial health premiums are often low to attract new customers, but sometime within the second year, they start creeping up. They'll continue to increase on every anniversary date of your policy. So, if you have no problem finding good coverage, switch when the payments start going too high.

• Skip the insurance agent from a particular company.

• Find a trade or professional association offering group health insurance.

• For a few bucks a month, pay the association dues and reap the health benefits.

Want to Slash Your Car Insurance Payments?

Here are some ways.

• Raise your deductible. Going from $200 to $500 cuts premiums by 15 to 30 percent.

• Drop the collision coverage when your car hits its fifth birthday. Warning! When you do, you'll no longer be covered for collision on rental cars.

• Install antitheft devices, and shave 5 to 15 percent.

• Airbags and seatbelts cut up to 30 percent.

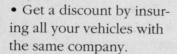

• Cut down on the weekly miles, and you'll knock off up to 25 percent.

• Get a discount by insuring all your vehicles with the same company.

• If you've got great health coverage already, drop the auto insurance medical payment.

• Cut unnecessary coverage such as towing and emergency road service. It's cheaper from AAA.

• Some states discount cars with anti-lock brakes.

Discounts Galore

Yep, you can get discounts on your homeowners insurance, but you have to ask. So, here's what will save you some bucks:

• alarm systems that ring directly into the appropriate agency—police, fire, ambulance

• deadbolt locks

• smoke detectors and fire extinguishers

• window locks

• no smokers in the house

• multiple policies with the same company

• mature owners

• brand new house

More Help

• If you can't find an association, contact an independent insurance agent.

• If you're 50 or over, check out American Association of Retired Persons (AARP) to see what they have. Go to www.aarp.org.

• Go to the library and find a book listing national associations, then get in contact with a few.

Here are some more tips:

• Raise your deductible from $500 to $1,000, and you can save as much as 25 percent.

• Don't insure your land along with your house.

Get Your Money's Worth

Here are some insurance traps for homeowners that'll get you if you're not careful.

• Buying coverage based on the market value can sting you later. *Always* buy insurance to cover replacement cost and protect yourself from inflation creep. It's not automatic, so ask for it.

• Too many claims can backfire. If the claim's for something small, pay for it out of pocket. Filing a lot of claims can get your insurance canceled, and you could have to pay up to three times the going premium rate for a new policy elsewhere.

Want to Get the Lowest Premium?

In the time it used to take to listen to one salesperson, you can now click through dozens of options online. And the more you comparison click, the more you can save. Here are some things you should know about e-insurance shopping:

• Your hunt will find insurance agencies, individual companies, and comparison companies that compare different companies for you.

• You'll be required to fill out online forms, but make sure they're on a secured site. All companies will send paper forms if you're more comfortable with them.

• If in doubt, go with a name you recognize. Tom, Dick, and Harry's insurance company is online, too, so be careful.

Chapter 9

Medical Money Savings

Where else can you step in the door and be charged $90 without being offered anything in return? It's your doctor's office, of course. You pay for the privilege of being there before they add anything else to your bill. These days, anything that's labeled *medical* comes with a huge price tag. But there are ways to slash through that tag and find a few savings.

Generics and More

You can save big money buying generic drugs, but you already know that. Here are some other money-savers no one mentions or offers unless you ask.

• Free samples are sometimes available from your doctor. If you're getting a prescription, your doctor may be able to give you a couple of weeks' worth of free pills if you ask.

• Split your pills. Many drugs can be prescribed in

various strengths for the same cost. If your pill is one of those, ask your doctor to prescribe the double-strength pills so you can split them in half.

Keeping Expenses Low

Don't just take that prescription and run to the closest pharmacy. Here are some savings tips.

• Ask your doctor the price of the drug before it's prescribed, and don't take "I don't know" for an answer. That information is only a phone call away.

• If you can't afford the medicine, ask for a comparable but less expensive drug. You may get an argument from the doctor, but don't back down.

• Many pharmaceutical companies offer free prescription drugs to people with financial need. For a list, visit the Pharmaceutical Research and Manufacturers of America Web site at www.phrma.org or call 202-835-3400.

A Few More Prescription Dollars Saved

Even if you're not a member of the American Association of Retired People (AARP), you can still score its prescription discounts. Other prescription plans, discounts, and insurances can be used with them. To take advantage of the AARP mail-order pharmacy, go to www.rpspharmacy.com or call 800-456-2277. If you are an AARP member (anyone age 50 or over can join), you can receive added benefits:

• Get a special AARP deal at any participating neighborhood pharmacy.

• AARP savings average about $9.46 per prescription (although savings vary by individual drug).

Call 800-439-4457 to enroll in the AARP Member Choice Program.

WWW Dot Online Drugs Warning

Online pharmacies are convenient but not necessarily the good deal you think you're getting. While the cost may seem low, you could be stuck filling out medical questionnaires for the online doctor's review every six months, to the tune of $60-$100 each time. Factor in those fees before you add up everything you think you're saving. If you can still save a little:

• Check out an online pharmacy's license with the National Association of Boards of Pharmacy at www.nabp.org or by calling 847-698-6227.

• Forget the foreign pharmacy sites. Their drug standards aren't always the same as those in the United States. What you're getting for your savings may not be what your doctor wants you to have.

Fast Fact

Save big money when you go to the hospital by taking your medicines from home. Hospital pharmacies can charge 10 times more than what you usually pay, so ask your doctor which meds you can bring, and make sure that gets written up in the doctor's orders.

Put Some Drug-Company Money in Your Pocket

You can help yourself to this gravy train by participating in clinical trials at a local hospital. Before you agree, you'll get complete information about the study, including possible side effects and benefits. By participating, you may get to try a new treatment that's better than anything currently on the market. These studies and their treatments usually include a thorough health examination without cost to participants. For more information, call the FDA's Office of Special Health Issues at 301-827-4460.

Keep Your Own Records

All it takes is a small note-book and pen. Then when the bill comes, you'll know if you actually received the treatment for which they're charging you an arm and a leg. If you're not sure of all the details of what the hospital personnel are doing, don't hesitate to ask. Here's what to record, including date and time:

• medications given (make sure you know what and how much)

• doctor visits, including doctor's name

• visits from other hospital personnel (excluding nurses)

• any treatment you receive

• all procedures (new IV, X rays, etc.)

• machines they drag into your room, whether they're used on you or not (and if they're not, note that, too)

Challenging the Bill Can Save You $$$

If you didn't get it, don't pay for it—not even a teenie, tiny co-payment. They're your dollars and you're entitled to keep them. Here's how:

• Request an itemized bill. It's your right.

• Check each item.

• Watch for double-billed items.

• Challenge discrepancies through the hospital billing service. *Put it in writing.*

• Send copies of any challenge to the hospital administrator and your insurance company.

• Refuse payment for questionable charges until the situation is resolved.

Virtually every hospital bill for inpatient stay has errors, and most resolu-tions will be in your favor if you challenge, especially if you took notes.

Free Medical Treatment

If you qualify for it, you could receive free medical assistance under the Hill-Burton Act. Here are the conditions:

• You must meet national low-income requirements. Find them at www.hrsa. gov/osp/dfer/obtain/ obtain.htm. Or, write or call: HHES Division, Room G251, Federal Office Building #3, U.S. Bureau of the Census, Washington, DC 20233; 301-457-3242.

• You must go to a medical facility that accepts Hill-Burton funds. Before you accept treatment at any facility, ask, or call the national 24-hour hotline at 800-638-0742.

• You must live in the Hill-Burton facility's service area, meaning you can't travel past two or three Hill-Burton facilities to go to another one that you'd prefer.

• You'll receive hospital financial aid, but you'll have to foot the entire doctor's bill yourself.

Hospital $$$ Facts

Here are a few ideas to consider when planning a hospital stay:

• Don't check into a hospital on Friday, because many routine procedures may not be performed until Monday. Early arrival could cost big bucks for very little medical care.

• Find out when the billing day for a hospital room begins, and check in after that time.

• A quick trip to an immediate care center could save you big bucks. But before you go, check with your doctor.

• Before surgery, ask if your procedure can be done on an outpatient basis. If it can, you'll save the hundreds of dollars you would have paid just for one overnight stay.

Save Big Medical Bucks

Here are some more tips to keep your money in your pocket:

• If your doctor prescribes tests not covered by Medicare and does not advise you of the fact, you are not required to pay.

• You can negotiate costs with your doctor. Many doctors, including surgeons, will lower the bill if you're willing to dicker.

Big Hint!

When your doctor sends you to a *specific* facility for tests, ask if it is a *self-referral*. This means the doctor or a family member has part ownership in the facility. These facilities are always more expensive than independent ones. New government rules

make this practice illegal, but there are exceptions.

Do I Really Need a Brain Scan?

You won't know for sure unless you ask. When a doctor orders a test, find out why. Some doctors love tests but don't think about your wallet.

Fast Fact

If you're seeking a second opinion, ask your doctor for copies of your medical records and X rays so these tests won't have to be repeated by the physician offering the second opinion.

• Find out how it relates to your condition or the procedure you're having. Will it help confirm or rule out a diagnosis or treatment?

• Use your head. If your doctor orders a brain scan for a stubbed toe, you may want a second opinion.

Free Medical Air Transportation

If your medical condition forces you to travel for care, the National Patient Travel Center arranges to transport eligible patients for no charge. If you need help, call 800-296-1217 or visit the Web site www. patienttravel.org.

Co-op Your Health Care

There's more power in a group than in an individual, so if there's no health-care cooperative in your area, start one. For more information on locating or starting a health co-op, contact: National Cooperative Business Association, 1401 New York Ave. NW, Suite 1100, Washington, DC 20005; 202-638-6222.

And here are a few good reasons why a cooperative will definitely cooperate with your wallet:
• discounts as much as 20 percent on dental, eye, hearing, chiropractic, and medical care
• discounted drugs and medical supplies
• waived Medicare deductibles
• waived Medicare co-payments

Look Out for Those TV Ads

You know—the ones that make it oh so easy to have your diabetic or asthma supplies delivered to your door. Well, here's what they're not telling you.

• Their medical supplies are more costly than the same supplies at your neighborhood pharmacy.

• You cover shipping and handling costs.

• Billing isn't always correct. It's not uncommon to find items on your bill that you didn't order or receive. They'll be billed to your insurance, though, and you'll get stuck with the co-payment if you're not careful.

You can get the same service that these ads offer from your local pharmacy, if you have a doctor's prescription. In the course of a year, you could save enough to pay for your next order.

Chapter 10

Your Golden-Age Money

You've spent a lifetime earning it and socking it away for your retirement or having it socked away for you by Uncle Sam. So read on to learn a little more about ways to keep what's yours safe and even make it grow.

Are You Raising Grandkids?

These tax credits may put some extra money in your pocket.

• Earned Income Tax Credit (EITC): If you work, you can reduce or even eliminate your federal income tax. Low-income workers can receive money from the government called "negative income tax." It can actually be paid in advance during the year.

• Child and Dependent Care Credit: This can reduce federal income tax of grandparents who pay for childcare.

• Child Tax Credit: This credit applies to federal taxes.

If you're raising three or more grandchildren, ask

about the Additional Child Tax Credit. Call your local IRS office for information, or go to www.irs.gov.

Become a Nonprofit Organization

This is an excellent way for retirees to contribute to a favorite cause. Pay yourself, as well as friends and relatives, as an employee. Your purpose could be charitable, political, or academic.

Once you've come up with a statement of purpose, you'll need to form a board of directors, file articles of incorporation with your state, draft bylaws, develop a budget and a strategic plan, and establish a record-keeping system. Find more information from the National Center for Nonprofit Boards at www.ncnb.org/askncnb/faq.htm. It may sound complicated, but it can be done on a part-time basis.

Such organizations qualify for state and local tax exemptions, so it can be worth the effort.

State EITC

These states have it, so if you live in one of them, call your state tax office to see if you're eligible for a little more personal income credit:

- Colorado
- Iowa
- Kansas
- Maryland
- Massachusetts
- Minnesota

- New York
- Oregon
- Rhode Island
- Vermont
- Wisconsin

Timesharing Money-Savers

It's a great investment, or so the salespeople claim. They're selling you a place to relax and enjoy your retirement. But here are some facts you should know before you hand over your money:

• A winter week somewhere warm is worth more than a summer week in the same place.

• You're often allowed to trade with other locations, but there's a fee, and the trade is not guaranteed.

Unfortunately, timeshares do not offer the best resale opportunity. Only 3.3 percent of all timeshare owners have been able to sell out in the past 20 years. So:

• Buy only in a development with a resale program.

• Sell with a company that takes fees only after the timeshare is sold.

It's Free!

Why pay $100 or more for your tax preparation, or even labor over it yourself and risk making big mistakes, when there are over 30,000 dedicated IRS-trained and certified volunteers standing ready to help you? AARP Tax-Aide:

• has 10,000 sites around the country

• is available to people of all ages with a middle or low income, especially those age 60 and over

• is available February 1–April 15

To find a site near you, go to www.aarp.org/taxaide.

Fast Fact

As it is today, and with no changes, Social Security will be able to keep up full payments to recipients, at pace with the cost of living, until 2037. After that, it will be able to pay only 72 percent of promised benefits.

Organize Your Financial Life for Free

This little money management beauty, *The Consumer's Almanac*, will help you organize your finances. It's free at www.pueblo.gsa.gov/cic_text/money/almanac/calmanac.htm. Here are some things you'll get:

• ways to organize your income, savings, living expenses, and credit obligations so you'll come out ahead

• how to plan for future needs

• how to incorporate long-range financial goals into your budget

• tips on managing credit

You'd Better Know Your Full Retirement Age

It used to be 65, but that's no longer the case. Does it matter? It sure does. The amount of your monthly Social Security payment is reduced if you retire before your full retirement age. Here's the chart.

Your Year of Birth	Your Full Retirement Age
1937 or before	65
1938	65 and 2 months
1939	65 and 4 months
1940	65 and 6 months
1941	65 and 8 months
1942	65 and 10 months
1943-1954	66
1955	66 and 2 months
1956	66 and 4 months
1957	66 and 6 months
1958	66 and 8 months
1959	66 and 10 months
1960 and later	67

The Dreaded Take-Away Formula

The earliest you can ever receive Social Security retirement benefits is age 62. No big deal, except that if you retire before your full retirement age, you won't get everything that's coming to you. Just take a look at these figures for someone reaching full retirement at age 67, to give you an idea of what you'll be missing. Ouch! It's quite a financial sting.

Your Age	Your Reduction
62	30 percent
63	25 percent
64	20 percent
65	13.32 percent
66	6.66 percent

Now here's the really ugly part! When you take a reduction for early retirement, it's permanent. It will never readjust up to the amount you would have received if you'd waited until 67 to retire. It will always stay reduced!

To view the entire Social Security reduction chart, go to www.ssa.gov/retire/agereduction.htm.

Just in Case You Didn't Know

Here are a few more interesting, and maybe profitable, Social Security facts:

• If your spouse has never worked, he or she can still receive a monthly check equaling half of your monthly Social Security retirement payment.

• Your spouse can begin collecting benefits at age 62, but they're subject to the full age requirement reductions, too.

• If your spouse is eligible for his or her own benefits, the higher between those benefits and half of yours will be paid.

Finding a Few Extra Bucks

Supplemental Security Income (SSI), administered by the Social Security Administration, stuffs a little extra cash into some pockets. Here are the qualifiers:

• You must be 65 or over, or blind or disabled.

• Financial resources cannot exceed $2,000 for individuals or $3,000 for couples. Homes, some cars, and burial funds up to $1,500 do not count against this limit.

• Monthly pensions can't exceed $530 for individuals or $796 for couples.

If you qualify, you'll get up to:

• $512 monthly for individuals

• $769 monthly for couples

And in most states, SSI recipients are also eligible for Medicaid health benefits. For more information, visit your local Social Security office or call the Social Security Administration at 800-772-1213.

Top Ten Pension Errors

These are mostly stupid mistakes, but they could mean money out of your pension pocket.

Fast Fact

The average American spends 18 years in retirement.

• Compensations such as commission, overtime, and bonuses weren't figured in.

• Calculation wasn't based on all your years with the company.

• Incorrect benefit formula, such as the wrong interest rate, was used.

• Wrong Social Security data was calculated.

• Company merged or went belly up, and there's

confusion over which benefits you qualify for.

• Basic personal information was incorrect.

• Account assets were improperly valued.

• Your employer didn't ante up.

• Someone made math errors.

• Personnel files weren't updated (to include changes such as marriage, divorce, etc.).

Now That You Know

Here are some pension safeguards:

• Know your plan. Get a copy of the rule book, called *Summary Plan Description*, and study it.

• Review your individual benefits statement and account information every time it comes in. Know your accrued (accumulated) and vested (absolute; not contingent upon anything) benefits.

• Keep a running pension file:
—where you've worked
—dates you worked there
—salary
—pension plan documents
—benefit statements

• Know your plan administrators, and notify them of changes that may affect your benefits payments (marriage, divorce, etc.).

Buried Funeral Costs

An unfortunate reality of the golden years is that they will come to an end. The average funeral can cost thousands of dollars, and those dollars are spent when you or your loved ones are at your most vulnerable. Being prepared can save you big bucks.

• Talk about funerals with family members ahead of time. Make sure your family knows your wishes.

- Do not be in a big hurry to make decisions or move the body. You have a few days to take care of this.

- Price shop for funeral directors, consultants, monuments, and caskets.

- Consider cremation. The burial of cremains is less expensive than burying a body. Or you can keep or scatter the ashes.

- Use a simple wood casket or cardboard casket, or even rent a casket if you are displaying the body before cremation.

- Plan a memorial service without the body present, and avoid embalming, a casket, and transportation of the body. Use a church, park, or community center for the service.

- Consider body donation to a medical school. In some areas, there may be no cost whatsoever, or only the cost of transporting the body. Cremated remains may be returned after scientific study, usually within a year or two.

- Handle all arrangements without a funeral director. A few generations ago, this was commonplace. Find out about the regulations and conditions concerning funerals in your state online at funerals.org/caring.htm.

- Be wary of prepaid funeral services. You could lose money if they go out of business before you die. Don't buy a casket ahead either, unless you plan to store it at home. Do you really believe some store is going to keep a casket in the back with your name on it for 30 years?